# MAKING PIZZA WITH MATH!

By Santana Hunt

Gareth Stevens
PUBLISHING

[ leveled
reader ]
math

Please visit our website, www.garethstevens.com. For a free color catalog of all our high-quality books, call toll free 1-800-542-2595 or fax 1-877-542-2596.

**Cataloging-in-Publication Data**

Names: Hunt, Santana.
Title: Making pizza with math! / Santana Hunt.
Description: New York : Gareth Stevens Publishing, 2020. | Series: Cooking with math! | Includes glossary and index.
Identifiers: ISBN 9781538245620 (pbk.) | ISBN 9781538245644 (library bound) | ISBN 9781538245637 (6 pack)
Subjects: LCSH: Mathematics–Juvenile literature. | Cooking–Juvenile literature. | Pizza–Juvenile literature.
Classification: LCC QA40.5 H86 2020 | DDC 510–dc23

Published in 2020 by
**Gareth Stevens Publishing**
111 East 14th Street, Suite 349
New York, NY 10003

Copyright © 2020 Gareth Stevens Publishing

Designer: Katelyn E. Reynolds
Editor: Kate Mikoley

Photo credits: Cover, p. 1 kikovic/Shutterstock.com; pp. 1–24 (gingham background) Mika Besfamilnaya/Shutterstock.com; pp. 1–24 (recipe background) A. Zhuravleva/Shutterstock.com; p. 5 4 PM production/Shutterstock.com; p. 7 Pressmaster/Shutterstock.com; p. 8 Danielle Balderas/Shutterstock.com; p. 11 Anastasia Izofatova/Shutterstock.com; p. 12 RTimages /Shutterstock.com; p. 15 Brent Hofacker/Shutterstock.com; p. 16 (mushrooms) GSDesign/Shutterstock.com; p. 19 panco971/Shutterstock.com; p. 21 (pepperoni) Hong Vo/Shutterstock.com.

Printed in the United States of America

Some of the images in this book illustrate individuals who are models. The depictions do not imply actual situations or events.

CPSIA compliance information: Batch #CW20GS: For further information contact Gareth Stevens, New York, New York at 1-800-542-2595.

# CONTENTS

**Boldface** words appear in the glossary.

# Pizza Party!

It's a pizza party! You can't make pizza without the help of math. A **recipe** helps too! Measuring, telling time, addition, and multiplication are just some of the math skills you might use in the kitchen. Let's get cooking!

Ask an adult before using the oven!

5

# Easy Cheesy Pizza

From peppers to **pineapple**, the toppings you can put on pizza are endless. But most pizzas need sauce and cheese! A recipe tells you how much of each **ingredient** to use. You will use measuring tools to make sure you've got the right amount.

You have a measuring cup that measures 1/2 cup at a time. Another measures 1 cup at a time. What's the best tool to use to measure the mozzarella cheese in this recipe? How many times will you use it? Check your answers on page 22!

# EASY CHEESY PIZZA

## Ingredients:

one ball pizza dough, **thawed**
one 8-ounce can of pizza sauce
2 cups shredded mozzarella cheese
1/2 cup **grated** Parmesan cheese

## Instructions:

1.  Take out pizza dough and allow to warm up to room **temperature**, about 1 hour. Heat oven to 400°F (204°C).

2.  Sprinkle some flour on the counter. Use a rolling pin to roll the dough into the shape of your baking sheet, which may be a circle or a rectangle. Place dough on baking sheet.

3.  Cover the dough with sauce. Then, cover the sauce with cheese.

4.  Bake in the oven for 17 to 20 minutes. Cut the pizza into pieces.

## Veggie Pita Pizza

Many recipes give a **range** of cooking time, such as 10 to 12 minutes. You can set a timer so you know when to check if your food is done! But, you also should keep an eye on the clock.

pita

11

It takes **patience** to wait for the cheese to melt in this recipe! You put your pitas in the toaster oven at 12:10 p.m. After 10 minutes, what time will it be? Use the clock to help you.

# VEGGIE PITA PIZZA

## Ingredients:

4 pita breads
1 jar prepared **pesto**
2 cups shredded mozzarella cheese
vegetable toppings like sliced tomato, sliced
sweet peppers, spinach, sliced onions

## Instructions:

1. Spread 1 tablespoon of pesto on each
   pita bread.

2. Sprinkle 1/2 cup cheese on each pita.
   Top with whatever vegetable toppings
   you like.

3. Place two pitas at a time into a toaster
   oven for 7 to 10 minutes or until the
   cheese is melted.

## Pizza Bagel

Most often, pizza feeds a party! But you might want to just make a little pizza for yourself. The recipe on page 17 serves one. You can use math to figure out how to make enough for friends too.

bagel

15

When making 1 pizza bagel, this recipe calls for 2 tablespoons of sauce. How much sauce do you need to make 3 pizza bagels? You can use addition or multiplication to figure it out!

$$
\begin{array}{r}
2 \text{ tablespoons} \\
2 \text{ tablespoons} \\
+\ 2 \text{ tablespoons} \\
\hline
?
\end{array}
\qquad
\begin{array}{r}
2 \text{ tablespoons} \\
\times\ 3 \\
\hline
?
\end{array}
$$

# PIZZA BAGELS

## Ingredients:

1 frozen bagel
2 tablespoons pizza sauce
2 slices mozzarella cheese
2 sliced white
   mushrooms

## Instructions:

1. Spread 1 tablespoon of pizza sauce on each side of the frozen bagel. Place one slice of mozzarella over the sauce. Add sliced mushrooms on top.

2. Put bagel on a microwave-safe plate. Heat in the microwave for about 2 minutes, or until the cheese is melted.

## Pepperoni Roll Up

Pizza doesn't have to be just a circle of dough with sauce, cheese, and toppings! You can think of new ideas and make pizza on crackers or in a sandwich. You may use pizza toppings in a tortilla—like this recipe does!

tortilla

19

Pepperoni can be **spicy**! If that's the kind you have for your roll up, you might want to use half as much pepperoni. How many pieces of pepperoni would you use?

$$8 \text{ pieces of pepperoni} \div 2 = \text{?}$$

# PEPPERONI ROLL UP

## Ingredients:

1 whole wheat tortilla
2 slices cheddar cheese
8 pieces of pepperoni
1/3 cup pizza sauce

## Instructions:

1. Place 2 slices of cheese in the center of the tortilla. Add pepperoni, placing pieces evenly on the cheese.

2. Microwave for 30 seconds. Roll the tortilla from one end to the other. Microwave for 1 minute.

3. Cut the roll up in half. Dip in the pizza sauce.

# Glossary

**grated:** made into small pieces by rubbing on a rough tool

**ingredient:** a food that is mixed with other foods

**patience:** the ability to wait calmly for a long time

**pesto:** a sauce made with basil

**pineapple:** a large, spiky fruit that grows on a tree and has sweet, yellow flesh

**range:** a series of numbers that includes the highest and lowest amounts possible

**recipe:** an explanation of how to make food

**spicy:** a flavor that causes a burning feeling in the mouth

**temperature:** how hot or cold something is

**thawed:** unfrozen

# Answer Key

**p. 8** the 1 cup measuring cup; use it 2 times

**p. 12** 12:20 p.m.

**p. 16** 6 tablespoons

**p. 20** 4 pieces of pepperoni

# For More Information

## Books

Baker, Linda R. *Learning Division with Puppies and Kittens*. New York, NY: Enslow Publishing, 2018.

McDougall, Nancy. *Ultimate Book of Step-By-Step Cooking & Gardening Projects for Kids*. London, UK: Hermes House, 2015.

## Websites

### 2nd Grade Math
*www.mathplayground.com/grade_2_games.html*
Find math games here!

### Recipes & Cooking for Kids
*kidshealth.org/en/kids/recipes/*
Discover more recipes you can make on this website.

# Index